Dr. Harold Taylor is one of America's most brilliant and progressive educators. As President of Sarah Lawrence College, he pioneered new scholastic methods for fourteen years, and resigned only recently to devote himself entirely to teaching and writing. He has just completed a tour of Europe and Asia, under the sponsorship of The Ford Foundation, where he conferred with educators, artists, political leaders, and students about problems of modern society.

Dr. Taylor is a dynamic and lucid spokesman for art education. He has a profound understanding of the creative process, its significance in daily life, and its importance to the cultural problems of our time.

"Art and the Intellect" and "Moral Values and the Experience of Art" are two of his most forthright and stimulating statements. Both were originally lectures delivered to the National Committee on Art Education at the Museum of Modern Art in New York. They should be read by educators and teachers everywhere and by all who are interested in the meaning of creativity and in man's spiritual survival.

These illuminating essays have the power of extending the cultural vision and understanding of the reader, whether student, teacher, artist or layman.

VICTOR D'AMICO, *Chairman*
The National Committee on Art Education

Director, Department of Education,
The Museum of Modern Art

ART AND THE INTELLECT

MORAL VALUES AND THE EXPERIENCE OF ART

HAROLD TAYLOR

Published for The National Committee on Art Education
by The Museum of Modern Art, New York

Distributed by Doubleday & Company, Inc., Garden City, N.Y.

"Art and the Intellect" was a lecture sponsored by the B. de Rothschild Foundation for the Arts and Sciences, and given at the 18th Annual Conference of the National Committee on Art Education; "Moral Values and the Experience of Art" was the major address at the 12th Annual Conference.

CONTENTS

ART AND THE INTELLECT

ART AND THE INTELLECT

The intellect is usually defined as a separate faculty in human beings — the ability to think about facts and ideas and to put them in order. The intellect is usually contrasted with the emotions, which are thought to distort facts and ideas, or contrasted with the imagination, which departs from facts.

As a result, it is often assumed that intellectuals are people who think, who have the facts and the ideas, and that the rest of society is composed of non-intellectuals and anti-intellectuals who don't. This is of course not the case, and it is possible to be an intellectual and not be intelligent, and to be a non-intellectual and think very well.

It is also assumed that there are basic differences between science and art, between scientists and artists; it is assumed that scientists are rational, objective, abstract, concerned with the intellect and with reducing everything to a formula, and that artists, on the other hand, are temperamental, subjective, irrational, and concerned with the expression of the emotions. But we all know temperamental, irrational scientists and abstract, cold-blooded artists. We know, too, that there is a body of knowledge in art. There are as many facts and ideas in art as there are in any other field, and there are as many kinds of art as there are ideas — abstract or concrete, classical, romantic, organized, unorganized, expressionist, surrealist, intuitive, intellectual, sublime, ridiculous, boring, exciting, and dozens of others. The trouble lies in thinking about art the way most people think about the intellect. It is not what they think it is.

This would not be quite so serious a matter if it were not taken so seriously, especially by educators and those who urge their views upon educators — that is, I suppose, the rest of mankind. If thinking is an activity which takes place in a separate faculty of the intellect, and if the aim of education is to teach people to think, it is therefore natural to assume that education should train the intellect through the academic disciplines. These disciplines are considered to be the subject-matter for intellectual training, and they consist of facts and ideas from the major fields of human knowledge, organized in such a way that the intellect can deal with them, that is to say, they are organized in abstract, conceptual, logical terms. It is assumed that learning to think is a matter of learning to recognize and understand these concepts. Educational programs in school and college are therefore arranged with this idea in mind, and when demands for the improvement of education are made, they usually consist in demands for more academic material to be covered and more academic discipline of this kind to be imposed. It is a call for more organization, not for more learning.

One of the most unfortunate results of this misunderstanding of the nature of the intellect is that the practice of the arts and the creative arts themselves are too often excluded from the regular curriculum of school and college or given such a minor role in the educational process that they are unable to make the intellectual contribution of which they are supremely capable.

When human knowledge is considered to be an organized body of fact and ideas, it seems to possess an independent reality of its own, it seems to exist by itself in time and space. In fact it does not. Knowledge does not exist until it is known by someone. It merely seems to exist because it can be recorded in symbols, words, and numbers. Few educators realize that dance, music, painting, design, and sculpture are forms of knowledge even though they do not express themselves in words. These arts can be talked about and facts can be assembled to describe their history and their characteristics, which is what most educators want to do with them, but that is not the most important thing about them as far as education is concerned. The important thing is the experience, the discipline and joy they give to those who engage in them and learn to value them. Such experience provides knowledge of a kind different from the knowledge expressed in words, but possessing a special kind of value. Only after the experience is gained is there any point in talking or writing about it, and even then, the purpose in talking and writing about that experience is to lead on to further experience and further understanding.

In spite of the truth of this, which seems so obvious, most colleges and schools allow their students to learn only *about* the arts through slides, lectures, textbooks, histories and appreciation courses, and not to engage in the arts themselves. That is, except in nursery schools, elementary schools, and in colleges for preparing students for teaching in nursery and elementary schools, where presumably it does not matter.

I wish to present the view that teaching people to think is not merely a question of training their intellects through the study of organized bodies of fact. This may very well teach them not to think but to memorize and accept what they are given, since all the work has been done for them and there is really nothing left to think about. The main problem is to teach people not only to think but to think for themselves, and to organize their own bodies of knowledge and experience. The intellect is not a separate faculty. It is an activity of the whole organism, an activity which begins in the senses with direct experience of facts, events and ideas, and it involves the emotions. The activity of thinking begins when an individual is impelled to think by the presence of questions which require answers for him. He begins thinking when he is involved in experiences which require him to place these in some kind of order. Until the individual becomes sensitive to experience and to ideas, until they mean something to him personally, or, to put it differently, until he becomes conscious of the world around him and wishes to understand it, he is not able to think creatively either about himself or about his world. His sensibility, his values, his attitudes are the key to his intellect. It is for this reason that the arts, since they have most directly to do with the development of sensibility, are an essential component of all learning, including scientific learning.

If we take this view, then education is itself an art, the art of teaching attitudes and values. An intellectual life begins for the student when his life includes intellectual interests of his own choosing, when he puts forth intellectual effort, that is, when he commits himself to learning because he wants to. Once an attitude is established, the student begins to organize his own body of knowledge and to conduct his own education. In this process, the teacher becomes an artist in the same sense that a writer or a painter is an artist. The teacher and the artist each expresses in his work his own attitude to life and the way he sees things, thus evoking a response in the student or in the observer. But the information being conveyed or "subject-matter" used by the painter or the teacher, although it may be important in itself and may be interesting in its own right, is primarily a vehicle for an attitude being communicated.

For example: one of the things we wish to create in students is an attitude to learning. We want our students to love learning, to be interested in ideas, to respect deeply the life of the mind. The subject-matter through which this respect is reached may be drawn from any field. But only when the attitude is present will there be true learning and true discipline, since without it, the student withholds his real self and makes no serious commitment. This is as true of science as it is of art; abstractions will not come to life until the student breathes life into them.

On the other hand, those who believe that the creative arts are central to education, and that the arts contain within themselves an intellectual discipline no less demanding than that of the sciences, must be very clear about what they mean and how they propose to apply what they mean. Too often it is considered enough to condemn the philistines and the dullards who do not understand the arts, to proclaim the unique virtue of art in education, turn as many students as possible loose in the studios and theaters, and hope for the best. They will express themselves, and everything will come out all right.

Cesar Barber of Amherst College spoke recently of the meaning of academic discipline by comparing it with the discipline of religion. The discipline of religion, he said, consists of performing certain rituals — going to church, praying, contemplating, fasting, reading the Bible, the Koran, or other text — the purpose of which is to become religious. The person becomes religious by undergoing the discipline, and the purpose of the discipline is to enable the person to be religious. Religion is the end, the discipline is the means, and the person willingly and devoutly undergoes a series of acts which he wishes to perfect in order to perfect his awareness of a god, to come closer to that reality. By engaging in these acts in the spirit of commitment he becomes religious.

The intellectual disciplines and the disciplines of art share this characteristic, and the purpose of their discipline is to achieve an awareness of ideas and values which otherwise would remain unavailable. It is therefore of the utmost importance to be clear that in those forms of education which concern themselves directly with the education of the emotions and with the development of sensibility there exist appropriate and adequate acts through which the ends may be achieved. It is not enough merely to feel, to express, to enjoy, to gesture. Ecstasy itself has its own necessary conditions and antecedents.

The art of writing provides an example. One way of considering the character of the young, the modes of their experience, and the character of the time in which they live is to ask what the young talk about in private, what they respond to most naturally and sincerely, what they read when they are free to read what they wish, what they write about in stories written, not for publication, but for their teachers. The written word makes public a state of mind, a state of consciousness which transfers from private to public expression a set of ideas and facts which would otherwise remain unavailable, both to the one who writes and to the one who reads. It is more than communication; it is the revelation to oneself, as writer, of things which have been hidden and are now forced into expression. On the other side, the side of the reader, the listener, or the observer, it is the revelation of one person to another, a personal communication in an otherwise impersonal world. This is one reason for deploring the loss of the old-fashioned habit of writing personal letters and, in education, for deploring the fact that high school and college students write so little, but instead take objective examinations by which they are asked not to speak but to grunt their approval or disapproval of a set of sentences or words.

The purpose of engaging the student in the act of writing is the same as the purpose of engaging him in true reading — to reveal to himself what it is he really thinks, what he honestly feels. He is not being taught to write poems, plays, stories, or essays so that he can publish them and be recognized or in order to "become a writer." That is technical training, undertaken to develop skills which may receive external rewards. In writing, the student engages himself in the discipline of expression; he is learning to know the discipline of the artist by becoming one. The task of writing is undertaken to enable him to become aware of the reality of art, to learn to recognize the truth that is in it, to enter more easily into this form of knowledge for the rest of his life. The disciplines of the sciences must be undertaken in the same spirit and with the same ends in view. The forms of discipline and the content of knowledge are different in the case of science, but the ends are the same. The ends, in this case, are to bring the student closer to the reality of science and to the scientist's way of thinking.

My plea is for the restoration of the personal element in modern life and in modern education at a time when everything is pushing us into collective states of mind and into the safety of anonymous opinion. We are being pushed into group thinking at a time when too many persons are willing to strip themselves of their individuality in order to become clusters of approved characteristics held in place by a desire to

loss of individuality

be liked and to be successful. Nor do I mean by the personal element the element of self-analysis. I mean the robust assertion of personal belief.

American culture has become fascinated by its self-analysis. Its novels are introspective, almost totally concerned with personal questions, with relationships, with personal manners; its theater and poetry have turned to the emotional content of human life and away from the bigger human issues; its social comment has to do with the nature of the American character. We have created a self-absorbed culture just now, concerned with psychological comfort, running for the doctor before we feel the chill. Our intellectuals are more interested in analysis than in construction, more in probing and reporting than in acting. It is a country of committees, surveys, and questionnaires. Whenever an action is proposed or an idea is held, it is first given a test to decide in advance whether the action will be approved or the idea accepted. When anything is suggested, a thousand little men run out to say why it can't be done or how it might fail. I don't know where they come from, but they're there. There is such a deal of peering, peeking, probing, and harassing on all sides that it is a wonder that anything gets done at all. As Christopher Fry once said, "Everywhere we hear the patter of tiny criticism . . ."

I learned in India recently an anecdote about three

tortoises which demonstrates the difficulties inherent in all action. These were three Indian tortoises — an older one, a middle one, and a small one. They were out for a walk, and the older one said to the other two, "Let's go have a cup of coffee." They discussed it for awhile and agreed to go. Just as they were going into a restaurant, the rain started to fall, and the older one said to the little one, "Son, would you mind running home and getting my umbrella?" The little one said, "Yes, I will, if you will promise not to drink my coffee." They discussed and agreed. The middle tortoise and the older tortoise went into the restaurant and sat down. Two years later the older one said to the middle one, "I guess he's not coming back. We might as well drink his coffee." Just at that point a piping little voice was heard from the front door saying, "If you do, I won't go."

In the middle of the welter of contemporary obstructions, it is important to remember that education is the means by which a student can find his selfhood. It is the way in which the student can find out what he believes, the way he can establish standards according to which he will live, the way he can find an image of himself and of his duties. The student must gain a sense of his possibility and of the range of action he knows he can undertake and that he wants to undertake. There is, therefore, a double task for the student — learning to do something useful for his society and his fellowman, and learning to know the range of possible human experience, that is, creating in himself a rich inner life, stocked with ideas and facts which are his own and which elevate the person and release him from ignorance and error.

But to achieve genuine individuality in the modern world one does not try always to be an individual. Individualism is achieved by trying to be honest with oneself, honest in one's judgments, tastes, preferences; individualism is an outcome of this effort — it is not its purpose.

The trouble is that most kinds of education are devoted to teaching students how not to be themselves, but instead how to cover up, how to gain enough knowledge, for example, in a survey course in Western civilization so that no one will ever know that you haven't read any of the authors or that you haven't ever really understood the works of art you were asked to observe. The usual kind of education — that is, the kind that is divided into courses, condensed into textbooks, put out in three lectures a week, tested by examinations, and rewarded by three academic credits a throw — is designed to give answers to questions which nobody asked and to inhibit the student in discovering his own truth and insight. The lectures and the texts do all that sort of thing for you. They provide a way in which the student can cover up his true self by finding a vocabulary acceptable to most people and a set of facts which are generally known among people generally considered to be generally educated.

Once this skill of covering up has been acquired, the student may never be called upon to say what he really thinks or feels at any point in his education or later life. This is what makes bores, and produces college graduates who are ignorant and dull, but successful and plausible. For a teacher who cares about teaching, there is nothing as exciting as students who are ignorant, who come to you uncorrupted by other people's knowledge of the things you know most about. I think it is wrong to judge students, especially when they are freshmen, by how much they know, since if they knew everything they should, there would be no need to be in college. That is what was wrong with Mr. Hutchins' college at the University of Chicago. It had a peculiar conception of the intellect. In order to get into the college, you passed examinations in all the things that they had to teach there, so that the best student was the one who passed all the tests for admission at the age of thirteen or so and didn't have to go there at all.

We need, then, a new philosophy for a new time; we need a redirection of our educational energies to create fresh ideas for the redirection of American society. I recommend for our consideration a definition of the elements in a new philosophy by Martha Graham.

Miss Graham said this: "There is a vitality, a life-force, an energy, a quickening which is translated through you into action, and because there is only one of you in all time, this expression is unique. And if you block it, it will never exist through any other medium and be lost. The world will not have it."

What Martha Graham has said, not only in this illuminating passage, but through her total attitude to life and through the expression of her art, defines an idea which must infuse any philosophy of education designed to release the talents of individuals. The forms of the dance which Martha Graham has created are free forms — that is to say they are forms newly created to express new truth which Miss Graham found impossible to express in any of the ways which dancers, choreographers, and playwrights had taken before her. Hers was not a rejection of the past, nor was it a refusal to accept her own tradition. The ancient dance forms of the East, the content of Puritan history, the classic mythology of Greece are all components of her art, an art which has transformed the past and transcended the limitations of a time and place far different from our own. The intellectual content of this art derives from sources as modern as Freud and as old as Sophocles. But there is an energy and a particular quality in American life which Martha Graham felt and which she made part of herself in her art and which she translated into action. This is the same force that Whitman recognized and which he, too, created new forms to express.

But the way to find that form and that energy which is truly our own — a form which is not European, not Russian, not anything but itself — is to learn how to be sincere and honest in feelings and judgment, how to be bold and courageous enough freely to proclaim a devotion or a belief, to recognize something which perhaps no one else will either like or approve, but nevertheless to recognize it, work with it, try it out, fearing neither success nor failure, courting no approval and posing no martyrdom, but doing everything in one's power to look at it freshly and honestly. This is the way to personal independence and personal freedom. It is also the way to a national goal which can transcend the confused and timid philosophy now infecting American life.

Nowhere is the confusion and timidity to be seen more clearly than in our public debates about education. All of us here today have had direct experience with one or another of the problems we face in American education. We are the ones who know about the shortages of funds, the weaknesses in teaching, the deficiencies in quality, and the lack of social energy. We are also the ones who know about the enormous resources of talent and idealism in American youth, their lively minds, and their willing hearts. We have seen at first hand the dedication of teachers who care;

we have seen the rich possibilities of intellectual and social advance in every aspect of American culture. We have seen some of those advances take place.

Yet the public debates on education reflect the aimlessness of our national policy, the same impulsive jumps from crisis to crisis, the same tendency to run from problems and talk in empty abstractions, the same refusal to come to terms with the real issues in the world of the twentieth century.

The real issues are not ideological. They are practical, and we would do very well to heed what General Marshall used to say: "Don't fight the question. Answer it." The practical issues have to do with obtaining disarmament, feeding the hungry, teaching the ignorant, building schools, housing the destitute, using science for human welfare, and doing all these things on a world scale at a time when the Soviet Union is doing everything in its power to make our answers to these questions seem ineffective and their own answers unbeatable. It is here that ideology, of course, becomes involved. But the choice between the ideologies of communism and democracy will be made by the people of the world not in terms of theoretical arguments but in terms of the practical results of the two systems.

We have become obsessed in this country with ideology and with fighting communism, and we organize our national and international policies around those of the Soviet Union. When they act, we react. We seem to have no plans and ideas of our own. The truth is that we would not be taking education as seriously or talking about it the way we now talk if it were not for the scientific and educational advances of the Soviet Union. In place of the bold line of progressive thinking which comes straight through from Jefferson, Tom Paine, Emerson, Whitman, Lincoln, Woodrow Wilson, Franklin Roosevelt, and John Dewey we are content to forsake our own tradition and to establish without thought, an equilibrium of economic and political forces by simply allowing events to happen as they please and accommodating ourselves to their results.

There are those who now tell us that progressive philosophy in social and educational matters has weakened our society and that we must turn back to conservative doctrines as we face the Soviet threat. The first thing we must do in education, we are told, is to stop being ourselves, repudiate progressive ideas, and turn back to European concepts, or to the second-hand copy of the European — the Russian. The second thing we must do, and have done, is to increase radically our support for the sciences, provide scholarships, fellowships, grants, research funds, and equipment, all under the necessity of the national defense and a competition with the Russians.

As a justification for remodelling our educational system, it is said that we need to spend more time, money, and energy on the "hard, scientific subjects and less on the time-wasting efforts of those in the arts and social studies who have blindly followed John Dewey in his concern for the individual child and for human values.

Let us accept the challenge in exactly the terms in which it is made. It is true that there are weaknesses in our educational system. In the effort to provide a democratic education for every child, according to his talents and needs, we have stretched our resources past the limit. There simply aren't enough good teachers to do what we are trying to do. In trying to match the growth of our population with an equivalent growth in its educational system, we have placed a burden on the existing system which it has not been able to carry. We have not spent enough money, although we have it at hand. We have spent it on other things — on motor cars, entertainment, luxuries, roads, and ten or twelve kinds of rockets which won't go off. If we had the money now spent on just one of those rockets, we could build a new school system almost anywhere.

It is also true that we have not asked as much of our students as they are willing and able to do, we *have* wasted time and energy in developing massive athletic programs, trivial extra-curricular activities, and a fun-and-games approach to a great many subjects. But is the cure for this to keep these main defects and add more blocks of science and mathematics while we allow the arts and the humanities to languish? Do we not need just as many educated men and women in the fields of public affairs, public health, poetry, social work, politics, theater, education, dance, medicine, public administration, painting, and government? Do we not need scientists and engineers who combine with knowledge and skill of a practical kind a sensitivity to human values, a sense of social responsibility, an understanding and appreciation of the arts? The widest sweep of imagination, the deepest level of intuition, the great command of insight are as necessary to the true scientist as to the poet or to the philosopher.

"Both science and art," says W. H. Auden, "are spiritual activities, not practical, whatever practical applications may be derived from their results. Disorder, lack of meaning, are spiritual, not physical, discomforts; order and sense are spiritual and not physical satisfactions. The subject and the methods of the scientist and the artist differ, but their impulse is the same, the impulse which is at work in anyone who, having taken the same walk several times, finds that the distance seems shorter; what has happened is that, consciously or unconsciously, he has divided the walk into stages, thus making a memorable structure out of what at first was a structureless flux of novelty."

It is with this conception of science and its relation to our culture and to art that we who are educators must be concerned. The growth of science is the one ultimate, unavoidable fact which has revolutionized the organization of knowledge and of society during the twentieth century. No country which fails to develop a system of education in which science is a major force and from which imaginative and devoted scientists emerge can hope to deal with the problems of a modern, industrialized, international society. But the way to achieve scientific and cultural strength and, therefore, to contribute to international leadership is not to convert our educational institutions to the production of science students. It is to raise the level of quality in all forms of education and to provide both scientist and non-scientist alike with the rich experience which only the enjoyment of the arts and sciences can bring. The scientific spirit is not opposed to the aesthetic, the moral, or the social. It is a spirit of enlightenment, of social advance, of creative thought. Let us not do it the dishonor of isolating it as a technique or trying to overcome it with flattery.

I wish to return to the topic with which I began — the definition of the intellect and its relation to art. There is a great deal of loose thinking about this. There are a great many inscrutable statements made by painters and sculptors, among others, about what they are doing. When narrowed down to something which can be recognized by the intellect, they say either, "I don't know what I'm doing," or, "I am doing something so private that I cannot tell you what it is." The unconscious has a new status and is often confused with creative imagination.

I would like to say one or two things about the unconscious and about the stream of consciousness in the work of the artist. I ask, "The stream of whose consciousness?" Some people's unconscious is a great dull area with some obvious things in it, which we all have, but everyone's unconscious is not equally interesting. The mere exposure of the unconscious does no honor to art.

I wish to speak, too, of the attitude which prevails among modern educators who are enlightened and who accept the arts and who, in some ways, have accepted the unconscious as the main source of human value. This has had an effect on a range of activities all the way from child rearing to the criticism of art.

For example, we are now finding in our colleges the first generation of understood children. The understood child has his own pathology and his own psychological attributes. I am thinking of the graduates of the private preparatory schools in the East and of a particular group within that community, the sons and daughters of the enlightened and understanding parents who raised them. I am thinking of the rebels within that group who, finding nothing to rebel against in the case of their families, with mothers and fathers who felt they could best exercise their rights as parents by understanding rather than judging, have come to identify the entire adult world of authority as "them," a group of people living on a separate planet. The young school hero of John Knowles' *A Separate Peace,* rejects the traditions and forms — those which are dominant in the family pattern of the well-to-do and the socially aware — and rejects both the rituals of the prep school and the attitudes of his family. Such a boy ridicules, in the novel, such things as the "Devon School Contact Sport Award, Presented Each Year to the Student Who, in the Opinion of the Athletic Advisors, Excels his Fellows in the Sportsmanlike Performance of Any Game Involving Bodily Contact." Among this particular group of sophisticated rebels is the gifted student who goes through the regular social system and achieves a privileged education until he learns to beat the system, goes to University, and then suddenly asks himself, "Is this all there is? Is this what life is really about?" — and proceeds quickly to his own salvation, having learned to reject what he could reject.

There is a psychological as well as social sophistication in young people who have been brought up with enlightenment, who understand the arts, who have received the psychological understanding of parents, teachers, and everyone else. This combines to produce a political conservatism and an acceptance of social reality and the kindnesses of other people just as they stand, without a wish to change society in any way but only to criticize it and to criticize such things as "them," mass culture, and mass education. You will recognize this rebel, or the member of the "shoe" (as it is called) subculture in J. D. Salinger, when his character Zooey speaks of how he has been brought up by his older brothers who told Zooey and his sister at a very early age "what it's all about," which amounts to how false everything is. Seymour and Buddy, the older brothers, are referred to in the following passage:

> These two bastards got us nice and early and made us into freaks with freakish standards, that's all. We're the Tattooed Lady, and we're never going to have a minute's peace, the rest of our lives, till everybody else is tattooed, too. . . . The minute I'm in a room with somebody who has the usual number of ears, I turn into a goddam *seer* or a human hatpin.

The dilemma for this sophisticated student is that often he is too intelligent to accept the values of his society, yet he needs desperately to belong to a community to which he can be loyal. He therefore rebels against the authority, and at the same time he is not quite sure he wants to go on being a human hatpin.

He has been taught to be critical of established values, but he has become tired of being himself all the time.

This brings me to the role of the unconscious in directing the thinking of enlightened educators. We have developed a progressive movement in which a whole array of modern devices in education which have been considered valuable and advanced have been put into action. We have developed in this progressive environment a student who is unable to rebel productively because there is nothing to rebel against. He is asked all the time to be himself. A great deal of the time the self he is asked to be is so unformed that he doesn't know what it is or how to be it. But this doesn't stop him from trying, and he develops a tremendous interest in himself and a tremendous interest in all those who are interested in him. On one hand, he asks for guidance and authority and intellectual discipline; on the other, he won't accept anything that anyone tells him on the grounds that that is just the way of authority and that is just discipline. He believes in the right of personal decision, free choice, and free speech, but only for other students, not for teachers or parents. As one student at a progressive college put it: "We would rather defend someone's right to say something than to listen to what's being said."

The progressive, advanced, enlightened, modern

student, who loves modern art, has a problem in that from birth, — or perhaps even in the preconception period — he has been treated with enlightenment and understanding. This has meant that the older line of authority which used to guide the child has been removed, and in a world in which he is not ordered around but told to choose his way he may stifle in an atmosphere of kindly overall approval. The intellectual discipline of which he is in search is unavailable. In an atmosphere of this kind, too thin in the oxygen of strong parental emotion, the young often feel a deep emotional fatigue from continually being forced to make their own decisions before they have had enough experience to be able to do so.

In the following passage, a student expresses her view of what has happened to those who have been educated in the arts and who have had an enlightened form of discipline. She refers to what she calls "the beat whole child":

With the present sophistication about the patterns of human behaviour, everyone is an authority on us. . . . As our lives unfold, each stage is greeted by the equivalent of a friendly yawn. . . . We are utterly recognizable.

Our unconscious life has been saluted with the same warm good will and enthusiasm as our conscious activity. The dark recesses of our unconscious, like our privacy, has been probed like garments at a fire sale. All the bite has been taken out of child rearing, literally and figuratively.

There are no retreats from this oppressive understanding. . . . Our lives are one big family album. When we feed, we're not hungry, we're oral; when we cry, we're not angry, we're rebellious; we're not spanked, we're rejected. The most beautiful accomplishment of the seven year old, the ability to love, is perceived as participation in some monstrous mythological event, the Oedipal dilemma.

With all this going on, it is natural for the modern, aesthetically sophisticated child to become clinical about himself and about others, including his parents. I have heard children of seventeen and eighteen discuss with their parents the proper way their parents should be handling them. Such children are often inclined to invent psychological difficulties and their solutions in order to satisfy a need for self-expression, and the possession of the right kind of psychological difficulties can attract its own social prestige.

The model for this type of young person is different from that of the regular high school student who has not been touched by the enlightenment of modern attitudes nor has been exposed to as many books and ideas which are considered "cool." But it is similar in its attitude of ingroupness and clannishness. It shows itself sometimes in a special form of intellectual and aesthetic snobbery about modern art, a snobbery o not being snobbish, or of feeling morally and aesthetically superior, and more intensely equal than anyone else.

This results in dismissing most of the other young high school students in the mid-West and all around the country as being either prep school types or teenagers, and coming down hard on something called mass culture and mass education — that is, what goes on in someone else's high school. A model for this new style of enlightened youth is the person who can wear jeans and a shirt with careless style; has read widely in all the modern novels — particularly the French; knows his way around the Village; understands women — or, if you are a woman, you understand men; loves folk singing, jazz and classical music, modern dance *and* ballet; is a liberal in international affairs; is critical of practically everything; hates The Bomb, Eisenhower, and Madison Avenue; and has got most of the major issues settled. It is also understood that, having settled these issues and received the feeling of satisfaction of being so right, the student need take no further action except to criticize the efforts of those who act on the issues.

I think it is fair to raise the question of the strength and vitality of our culture now that we have these sources of enlightenment in modern psychology, in modern educational attitudes, and in modern art. I think it is fair to ask what the teachers of art and the

teachers of the arts in general are doing about it.
Sometimes I feel that many teachers are doing very
little about it, except to encourage people to paint and
sculpt in any way they wish. If a plain citizen questions the principle that the impulse of the subcon-
scious is the ultimate determinant of true art, he is
often quietly ignored in the way one has with the par-
tially deranged. If an educator stands up and says, "I
don't think that slopping paint around or playing with
plaster is doing very much for the intellectual development of the student," he is considered to be a hidden agent of Admiral Rickover.

We need to face the fact that there is a great deal
of romantic nonsense talked about what the practice
of the creative arts does and can do for humanity and
the country at large. We need to be clear about the
way in which the discipline of the visual arts can become a means of learning how to think, how to see,
and how to understand, at a higher level of understanding, many things other than art. Science, for example. We also need to remember that once the student has become involved in the practice of an art
there are many ways in which the culture in which the
art exists can be understood and must be understood
and that the student must learn to profit from know-
ing in some detail the history, economics, politics, and
philosophy of a civilization which supports cultural
values and a concern for the arts. Again, the gap be-

tween science and art is unfortunate. The gap between art and a knowledge of social, political, and economic circumstances is equally unfortunate.

I am struck with the fact that those who have the most opportunity to know these things and to do something about them are quite often those who feel that the responsibility to act belongs to someone else, usually an administrator. We are all responsible, both for our own students and for our country. I do not propose that we mount an effort to defeat the Russians with superior works of art or a more intense concern with aesthetic values. I do propose that we work where we are to persuade our students to engage themselves in the enterprise of learning, through the arts, to develop a sensibility and a means of judging good from bad, true from false, and beautiful from ugly.

When we have a culture in which our students, their parents, and our school and college graduates hold to standards of sensibility, then we have a culture of which we can be proud, and which, in terms of world opinion, can command its own respect. Our government does not yet realize that our cultural policy must be one, if it is to be effective, which makes no boast of its cultural virtues, which makes no boast that this system of political democracy produces better art than any other, but one which just quietly allows the works to speak for themselves.

Why then, in a country so interested in human values, so concerned for education, so full of idealism and opportunity for every kind of cultural advantage should there be a confusion of aims and a lack of intellectual purpose? Why, as a friend of mine asked recently, should students sometimes starve in the midst of plenty? To which my friend answered, quoting the famous Zen Buddhist story:

> It is too clear and so it is hard to see.
> A man once searched for a fire with a lighted lantern.
> Had he known what fire was,
> He could have cooked his rice much sooner.

This is your opportunity. You know what fire is.

MORAL VALUES

AND THE EXPERIENCE OF ART

MORAL VALUES

AND THE EXPERIENCE OF ART

I begin with a question set by Socrates, drawn from Plato's *Republic*.

"Do you hold the popular belief that, here and there, certain young men are demoralized by the private instructions of some individual sophist? Does that sort of influence amount to much? Is not the public itself the greatest of all sophists, training up young and old, men and women alike, into the most accomplished specimens of the character it desires to produce? When does that happen? Whenever the populace crowds together at any public gathering, in the Assembly, the law courts, the theatre, or the camp, and sits there clamoring its approval or disapproval, both alike excessive, of whatever is being said or done; booing and clapping till the rocks ring and the whole place redoubles the noise of their applause and outcries. In such a scene what do you suppose will be a young man's state of mind? What sort of private instruction will have given him the strength to hold out against the force of such a torrent, or will save him from being swept away down the stream, until he accepts all their notions of right and wrong, does as they do, and comes to be just such a man as they are?"

What sort of private instruction will have given him the strength to hold out against the force of such a torrent? To prevent him from becoming a cipher, a type, a creature without a personal identity?

To this we can only answer that whatever else we do as teachers and educators, our central concern must be to help the young to find a personal identity, and a philosophy by which they can live. To do so, it is necessary for each of us to discover within ourselves and within the world which surrounds us a set of principles and aims which can give direction to our own lives and to the lives of our students.

For it is true, as Socrates says, that the public itself is the greatest of all sophists. A sophist is a man who makes the worse seem the better cause, a man who makes arguments, not to establish the truth but to make a lie seem plausible. This is something which the public does, whether we like it or not. In contemporary American life, there are so many public pressures which bear down on the individual American citizen, that it requires a serious and sustained effort of will to think and even to feel independently. It requires a continuing reaffirmation of moral courage to express independent conclusions once they have been reached. It is as if all the pressures of modern life were conspiring to crush the individual and to make him conform to a stereotype set by governments and public officials.

Yet these very pressures, once they have been clearly seen as threats to our individual independence, may produce their own reaction, may make us rise to meet their challenge. There is no better way to arouse the American citizen than to order him around or to tell him what to think. Although there are many people in this country who would like to organize us more thoroughly and tidy up the freedom we have by a little more control, we still reserve the personal right to plunge our own way into our own mistakes and discoveries, in art, philosophy, education, or politics, and we suffer fools to tell us what to think and what to do, because in this country when a fool tells us what to do, we don't necessarily have to do it.

We must also remember that it is only in response to a challenge or a threat that we are forced to state our principles and to stand on them. No one is interested in gentle declarations of virtue. Everyone is interested in strong and vigorous statements of principle when principle is challenged by attack. The search for a personal philosophy begins when we realize the need for one, when we see clearly that unless we believe deeply in ourselves and our values, we will lose our own individuality.

One of the primary tasks of the teacher in America today is to reach the individual consciousness of our students, to penetrate beneath the surface of the clichés and slogans which cover the public mind, and to set in motion those spontaneous and fresh insights which lead toward personal truth and personal value. This is the beginning of philosophy and of true education, and although we cannot hope and dare not try to give to our students a single set of values and a single pattern of knowledge which everyone must accept, when we succeed in moving the private consciousness into a condition of eager inquiry, we have begun the process towards a philosophy which they themselves will complete.

I am tired of hearing that moral values have disintegrated. I am tired of hearing that the modern world has deprived life of its meaning, that the ideals of classical civilization have been shattered. I am weary of people who claim we are lost, bewildered, frustrated, neurotic, decadent, uncertain, threatened, immoral, corrupt, and generally doomed. Some people are. Some aren't.

We are, after all, living in our own world, in our own time, with our own values. It is, above all, an interesting time, if a little more dangerous than usual, and if its values are not identical with those of the upper class, or philosophical set, in classical Greece, or are not identical with those of the emperors, soldiers, consuls, and working writers of the early Roman period, or with the ecclesiastical group of the medieval period who burned their heretics or shut them up in other ways for the ultimate benefit of human welfare, or with the nineteenth-century group of bankers and merchants who got along by keeping the workers in a state of economic and social insecurity, I find that I can face this fact cheerfully, and look around for some new values which can work a little more happily for everyone than the old ones used to do.

The disintegration of older values in favor of new has been going on for the past two thousand years. In the twentieth century we are much more self-conscious about it, and with an acute awareness of our own history and the reasons we have come to be as we are, we have fallen into doom-ridden ways of talking about the certainties of the past and the horrors of the future. The only reason the past is certain is that it is dead, and this I consider too great a price to pay for certainty.

We have, among many others, Mr. Toynbee's warning that history is working out its present phase at our expense, and we have Mr. Toynbee's assurance that when civilizations appear to be at their most healthy, prosperous, and blooming, they are actually rotting away at the core and are about to begin a radical decline. Those ignorant of this fact, or those who protest against it, are simply unaware of the inner dynamic of history. In other words, the rosiest apple contains the biggest worm.

On this point Mr. Toynbee is either wrong or right.

In all questions of this kind referring to the present
and where it is going, no philosopher or historian has
better than this fifty per cent average, although many
philosophers can be much more solemn about it than
the ordinary scholar who makes predictions about the
future as a professional occupation. Since Mr. Toynbee's idea cannot be verified except by going on living
in order to see what will happen, I suggest that, for
the time being, we simply turn his theory around the
other way, and by a happier logic, which has just as
much chance of being true, we all accept the idea that
when civilization seems to be at its worst stage, it is
actually at the beginning of its best and most promis-
ing. In this way, we can all face the future (at least
for the time being) with grace and moderate joy, and
with an amount of historical dignity equal to that of
Mr. Toynbee.

At the same time, it is of first importance to recognize that our present crisis has special qualities, and
that it is not just another period of the sort which
followed wars in the past. The prime fact is that for
the first time, we have the means, and to some degree
the will, to destroy the whole of contemporary civilization. Our age is marked by its use of power, vio-
lence, terror, and intimidation as the standard means
of settling social conflicts, with a sharp decline in the
use of persuasion, appeal to moral values, and respect for personal rights. It is of course marked by an

enormous increase in the development of new ways of bullying people into thinking required thoughts through the mass media and political coercion. Its favorite words are confusion, tension, and action. It is marked by the growth of politics to an overwhelming size in the scale of human concerns. But perhaps more significant than any of these things, and in large part as a result of them, it is marked by a continuous assault on the privacy and the moral confidence of the free-thinking individual. The purpose of the assault is to drive everyone into line, to force agreement to policies, ideas, and acts which have been determined by state, public, or group authority.

There is an ultimate privacy of the moral conscience which is at the center of all personal values. If that privacy is invaded by force, coercion, or threats of coercion, the effect is to dry up the flow of action and ideas from which new moral values come. With the loss of that privacy, moral and intellectual self-confidence is lost as well, and the individual hesitates, examines, analyzes, and is silent. It drives the individual within himself, and detaches his inner life from his outer action. He then says things which he does not mean, and under compulsion, does things which he does not mean, and which produce an inner conflict and a secret embarrassment. The destruction of the human personality begins to be possible when that privacy is threatened, and the destructive element in social and political life begins to damage the individual when a society allows this threat to become real.

Some of these threats are to be found in the attacks on the twentieth-century child through education. Sometimes the attacks are made under Communist auspices, as in Eastern Europe, sometimes under Fascist auspices, as in Spain and Argentina, at other times under organized bigotry, as in the United States. We should remind ourselves of the identical pattern to be found in each instance of attack on the child's mind and personality. The first act of an authoritarian group, whether communist, fascist, or just plain patriotic, after it has seized power and control of the Army and police force, is to capture the universities and the schools. Later come the capture of the artists and the writers. The pattern in all instances is simply this: tell the student what is valuable, what to think, what to do, and by psychological, political, or even physical means coerce him into believing that what he has been told is true. Whether or not he feels it to be true is not important. He must be required by the educational authorities to make the correct public response to questions asked as to what is true, good, and beautiful.

This is the basic issue in the question of moral values and education. We who believe in democratic education know what are the moral values which we want our children to accept and to fulfill in their lives. We want them to be honest, fair-minded, just. We want them to enjoy their lives, and to have a sense of purpose about the way they live and the experiences they choose. We want them to be sympathetic and generous in their attitude to other people, to other cultures, and to other countries than their own. We wish them to be sensitive to the beautiful and the ugly, in actions and objects alike. We want them to believe in individual rights and human freedom, and to have a breadth of knowledge and a way of finding the knowledge they do not have. We feel that it would also help if they were rational.

There are a great many ways in which these qualities are learned, and a great many different kinds of people who show them — composers, poets, scientists, farmers, workers, teachers. This is not necessarily a matter of college education, since the qualities of the desired kind seem to develop equally well in other places.

Values are learned, not always consciously, by the particular set of situations in which people spend most of their time, by the direct and indirect personal influence of parents, teachers, friends, and employers. The value of things and of ideas is learned only by the immersion of the individual in the stream of human relations which make up his daily life. The value of democracy is not learned merely by the study of its history or its character, but by learning what it feels like to be democratic. The value of a painting or a poem is not learned by hearing it described and praised, although that may help, but by responding to it personally. Unless the personal response is present, nothing has happened.

The beginning of moral values is in the child when he first explores his talents and desires. His mind and the rest of him all grow together as he plays with clay, rides his tricycle, learns to read, and wrestles his friends. When we think of children we think of them in terms of their possibilities, their needs, and their efforts at understanding. A genuine sense of wonder exists in each child and each one, if he is given a chance, asks about the origin of practically everything, and why things happen as they do. The child continually looks for values and for truth, and his search leads him to the important issues. These are the issues of what is good and what is bad, what is beautiful and what is not, and what is true and what is false. He asks for help, and wants to know from us what answers we can give him.

We cannot avoid giving answers. But we can avoid forcing the answers upon him as a form of revealed truth. We can also avoid cutting up the answers into different departments of knowledge, and classifying what he learns as science or art. We tell him as much as we can about what he asks, and let it go at that. It is only when he becomes enmeshed in an educational system that he learns that there is a difference between science and art, poetry and fact, knowledge and values. When we are faced with the child in the raw, we try to teach him to live in his world by seeing the relations between one thing and another (philosophy), understanding how to deal with himself and other people (psychology), what are the names and descriptions of various things (science), how to enjoy life (the arts), how to exert influence on his parents and other people (social science), how to count and do abstract thinking (mathematics), how to imagine people and situations (literature), and what are some of the more desirable ways to behave (the humanities).

I suggest therefore that we look at the whole of education as a series of different experiences, some of them more useful and interesting than others. Children and adults will continue to have experiences whether we wish them to or not. Socrates has said that the public is the greatest of all sophists, and is capable of the highest degree of corruption. He could also have said that the public, or society, is the greatest of all educators, since it surrounds the child and the adult with continual experience from which the individual learns.

The difference between a school or college and all the other institutions of society is that the particular kind of experience we give to the student is selected in terms of an idea about what we want the child to become. The difference then between the school and society is that the ultimate concern of the school is with moral value, or, with the idea of what the child ought to become and what man ought to be. Society as an ongoing process is concerned with such matters only occasionally, when, for example in America, it breaks out in a rash of investigating committees which, without bothering to find out what is moral and what is immoral, tend towards the enjoyment of investigation for its own sake, and before long I hope will produce a congressional committee to investigate investigating committees. The educational system is the instrument through which the basic values of a given society are transmitted and recreated from generation to generation.

Now I would like to raise the single question: what is the basic value in our American society which we want to transmit? What single item can be said to distinguish our value system from any other? If we have to choose one single item, it must be freedom. It is because of the ideal of freedom that we have organized our particular form of democracy, since the political structure of any society is modified or formed to support the demands which the people make for the attainment of certain values. Because of our good fortune in the variety of interesting people of all types, colors, sizes, and attitudes, who have come to this country from the start, and because of the variety and richness of the social and natural resources with which the country has abounded, in order to realize to the full the potential which has always existed here, we have *needed* the idea of freedom as a social instrument to be used for our full development.

The next question I would ask is therefore: what single moral value among all others do we need to teach, through our social institutions and through our educational system? The answer I am forced to make, if what I have already said is true, is that we must teach our children to be free, and to value freedom as an attitude to life and to themselves. At this point we need to know what we mean by freedom and how we go about teaching it.

As one aspect of the self-consciousness of the twentieth century, we have come to be interested in the actual development of the human personality, and have formed new theories about human nature. The classical view of human nature holds that the individual human being is identical throughout the whole of the species, he contains a mind composed of a mental substance in about the same way that an egg contains a yolk. Although, in the classical view, the body may change and may vary from person to person, and may occasionally get the mind into trouble, it has only incidental relations with the mind, and thus has little to do with education or the development of the personality. For this reason, a major part of traditional education consists in wrestling with the body, keeping it out of the way, curbing the emotions, trying to make students learn in spite of themselves, and trying to keep the natural desires of the human being from interfering with the intellectual processes.

A modern theory of human nature is much more complicated. It accepts, for example, the influence of social environment on the personal character of the individual. It accepts the existence of an area of the unconscious as a significant part of the total human personality. It assumes that there is a direct relationship between childhood experience and character in later life. It accepts the fact that motivations and talents are different from person to person, and different in each person at different times in his life. In other words, it accepts as observably true that each individual human being is a special case, and that if education is to be effective, it must deal with the emotional, the intellectual, and the social needs of the individuals it is serving.

It is with a modern theory of human nature that I wish to deal, since it is so closely related to modern theories of education and of art. A large part of the experimental work which has been carried on in modern education has had to do with the various ways in which children can learn to become free, and in becoming free, can learn to discipline themselves to the needs of others, to the needs of their society, and to personal needs of their own. We know a great deal more than we used to know about the relation of the creative arts to the emotional development of children, and we know enough to say that creative work in the arts has a generous contribution to make to the full maturing of the individual, or, as we often say, to the development of the free personality. By this I mean a personality which is capable of reacting spontaneously, freshly, and independently to a new situation as it emerges in experience.

Political, social, and economic freedom are of course directly related to personal freedom, and involve freedom for the individual to choose among a rich variety of alternatives without the restrictions produced by hunger, class stratification, authoritarian rules, poverty, and economic insecurity. But once external freedom has become such that the individual citizen can share actively and without inhibition in the formation of public policy, the matter of personal freedom comes up again, this time in the form of a question: how can the individual learn to use his freedom in making discriminating choices among personal and social alternatives? If there is no one to force him to accept rules about what is good and bad politics, what is good and bad conduct, what is good and bad art, how does he make up his mind?

The answer is that he has to learn how to do it as

a part of his total education. To be free in the sense
of being able to make independent choices means
that the free person must know a great deal, must be
sensitive to a wide variety of experiences, and must
have enough confidence in his own judgment to as-
sert it and to learn how to correct it through further
experience. It also means that he must have learned
to respond to other people and other ideas, different
from his own, rather than reacting against them, and
that he has learned to accept differences as natural
rather than as a threat to himself and his whole style
of life.

We also know enough about the authoritarian personality to say that those who are opposed to freedom for others and who want a controlled and ordered society have a standardized way of behaving
towards many different kinds of situations, all the
way from child-training to modern art. Such individuals show hostility to all groups and kinds of people who are different from themselves, consider the
world a dangerous and threatening place, place ex-
ceptional emphasis on social power and social status,
and are both socially and personally insensitive to the
needs and wishes of others.

The extraordinary fact is that there is such a close
relation between a hatred of liberalism in political
and social terms, and a hatred of modern art, modern
education, modern literature, and modern life in gen-

eral. It is not hard to understand why people object to politicians whose ideas they do not like, or who might involve them in higher taxes, or why the people who detest state control of anything also object to price control. But why there should be such incredible outbursts against modern art, why abstract painters should be considered more likely to be subversive than the realists, why representational sculpture should be considered more patriotic and more American than mobiles, why political criteria should be used to judge works of art of any kind, requires a great deal of understanding. It also requires a great deal of patience on the part of the artists, museum directors, and teachers who are attacked.

What has the modern artist done to deserve the violent epithets of Congressmen, the President of the United States, war veterans, conservative sculptors, clergymen, and museum directors? Essentially what he has done is to say — here is the way I see contemporary reality, this is the way I wish to work, these are the things I present for you to see, this is what I believe about art, this is what I have learned, I intend to go on working this way, consider it, look at it, enjoy it, with my compliments. As far as I can see, the conduct of the artist is impeccable, he makes no claims except through his work, he threatens no one.

The conduct of the observer, however, when he comes to the gallery or to the museum is a matter for the observer to determine for himself. If he screams with rage, if he feels himself threatened, insulted, or badgered, if he shouts that contemporary reality is not like that, if he cries for the Sistine Madonna, if he calls for the police, this reveals something in him, not in the artist or the art. For the majority of others, that is, those who don't actually go to the galleries and the museums, the act of looking at sculpture, architecture, and paintings themselves is not a necessary preliminary to denunciation. Modern art along with modern education is said to be corrupting, enervating, decadent, and Communist, because, as one happy little band of critics put it, it is dangerous "to the whole philosophy of national normalcy."

Certainly. It is dangerous to rigidity, smugness, conformity, and sterility. It starts from different assumptions, and moves to different conclusions. It refuses to take its orders from outside the areas of aesthetic judgment, or from any other source than the individual creative idea. It asserts the value of free expression, in whatever medium and in whatever form the artist finds valid and creative. When it fails, it fails for its own reasons, not for the reasons assigned to it by those who reject its right to exist.

Yet within the past two months, bitter denunciations of modern art and modern artists have been made on exactly the opposite grounds. The most recent one came from a Congressman who, taking the present Soviet line on "formalist" art, bundled together a variety of museums and galleries along with the artists themselves, as the conveyors of "distortion, frustration, and a spirit of rebellion," in addition to acting as conveyors of Soviet and Communist propaganda. Included among those accused of being modern was one rather conservative museum whose director had himself denounced modern art just recently on the grounds that it was (a) rejected by the public, and (b) was having a widespread pernicious influence.

But in the general denunciation of pernicious influences, I believe that the National Sculpture Society's recent statement about politics, art, sculpture, and corruption makes the most important contribution to the literature in the field. It is of especial significance for our discussion. It reads, in part:

"In many of our schools and colleges, the students are being systematically indoctrinated in the philosophy of imaginative anarchy in the creative arts. . . . Unfortunately, by destroying an ideal of beauty, endeavor, and discipline in the artistic expression of a people, the very foundations upon which this national achievement rests are being undermined. The so-called "modern" artists claim that they represent the New Age, and the tremendous changes it has brought. We most heartily repudiate this claim, in the name of the sound, normal American people."

It is here that I come at last to the middle of our subject. We are now thoroughly involved in the matter of moral values and the experience of art. The experience of art is one which quickens the human consciousness to a greater sensitivity of feeling and a higher level of discrimination among ideas and emotions. There is not just one kind of art which lends itself to this experience, whether modern or traditional, painting or design, sculpture or literature. The art objects themselves are the occasions on which individuals, either the artist who made them or the observer who recreates them, can move more freely into areas of experience which were formerly unknown.

We cannot destroy the idea of beauty or of truth except by crushing the artists themselves, or by forcing their expression into insincerity by the demands we make for "normality" and conformity. The experience of art, for the child in school and for all of us, is an experience through which we can gain an insight into what it means to be free in emotional response and free in the choice of ideas. The experience of art is a way of enriching the quality of human experience, and of reaching a precision in the choice of values. It is a particular kind of experience which requires for its fulfillment a discipline, freely undertaken, a knowledge firmly grasped, a heightened consciousness, and an intensity of interest in the creative and imaginative aspects of human life. It is not an experience which takes the artist out of the material world or out of the context of his society, but an experience which moves through contemporary reality into newer levels of awareness of what human society is.

The moral value of art lies in this process of discovery, and in this contribution to the richness of human experience. It draws attention to other values in the world than those connected with material, social, or political power. The experience of art leads each of us into discussion of ultimates, into questions of truth, into serious philosophy, since the response evoked in each of us becomes part of our way of looking at the world and part of our stated and unstated vocabulary or response.

The ideals of the spirit of humanism are carried, not in manifestoes, catalogs, or proclamations, but in the hearts, minds, and hands of the creative artists. Through them and through their work we find a continual reassertion of the invincibility of the human intelligence in its continual struggle with ignorance and bigotry. This provides its own proclamation of freedom, freedom for the imagination, for the reason, and for the human personality. Those who catch the meaning of this freedom, through their experience with art, possess an antidote against despair and a weapon against oppression.

We teach the meaning of freedom when we teach the young to explore the world of imagination and art. We give the private instruction which can enable young men and women to hold out against the torrent. We help to restore the intellectual vitality, the self-confidence, the moral dignity of the contemporary individual by the imaginative reconstruction of human experience. In doing so, we can show that human life is greater, more noble, more wide-ranging in its possibilities than the particular embodiment it now takes in the politics and disorder of our present moment.